Heaven, Who Will Make It?

PASTOR SEYI OGUNORUNYINKA

The ultimate goal of every child of God should be to make heaven, the place of eternal rest that our father has prepared for us.

In **John 14:2** Jesus tells us, **"In My father's house are many mansions; if it were not so I would have told you, I go to prepare a place for you"**.

Heaven is a place of place and joy with none of the problems that we face here on earth. It follows that every child of God should be desperate to get there. It is therefore baffling that so many Christians have placed their focus on building up treasures here on earth, to the detriment of preparing to enter what should be their eternal home. The things of this earth are only temporary and will eventually pass away. Consequently, our primary focus should not be on this world, but on heaven, our ultimate destination.

It is God's earnest desire that we all make heaven and he tells us in his word the things that we need to do to make sure that we get there. In this book, we will look at the mistakes that men have made in the past that caused them to miss heaven and we will learn about the changes God desires that we make in our lives to qualify us to inhabit the mansions he has prepared for us.

I pray that as you read this book and apply the principles to your life, you will be counted amongst those who make heaven.

Contents

1. Chapter 1   1

2. Chapter 2   8

3. Chapter 3   16

4. Chapter 4   24

5. Chapter 5   31

6. Chapter 6   38

7. Chapter 7   44

8. Chapter 8   52

    54

Chapter 1

THE BURDEN OF GOD

Most of us would agree that the whole essence of our Christian race is to make heaven. So if you call yourself a Christian but you are not sure within yourself that you are going to end up in heaven, then you have a lot of work to do.

Many people come to church but very few of them are heaven-bound. When they come to church they hear the word of God but as the word comes in through one ear, it goes out through the other. That is why so many so-called children of God are living in sin and are engaged in practices that are abhorrent to God. They are like the people Jesus described in the parable of the sower and the seed in **Luke 8:5-15**. Verses **11-14** read,

"The seed is the word of God. Those by the wayside are the ones who hear; then the devil comes and takes away the word out of their hearts, lest they should believe and be saved. But the ones on the rock are those who, when they hear, receive the word with joy, and these have no roots, who believe for a while and in time of temptation fall away. Now the ones that fell among thorns are those who, when they have heard, go out and are choked with cares, riches, and pleasures of life, and bring no fruit to maturity."

If someone who was raised in a Christian home by Christian parents passes away, and if that person was active in church and professed to be born again, then as a matter of course, a Christian wake keeping world be organized and a sermon would be preached with reassuring words on how the deceased is now in heaven. The truth, however, is that if that person died in sin, then hell and not heaven will be his final destination. It does not matter which church he attended, how long he was born again or what position or role he held in the house of God; it does not matter how much he professed to love God, or how he did his work. For as long as he did not practice the word that he heard in church, then he will not make heaven.

The question of who will make heaven is a burden to God; it is a burden that he carried since the beginning of time and it is still with him to this day. It may sound like blasphemy to say that God has a burden or a problem. Some might say that it is profane, irreverent and even a sacrilege to say that the omnipotent God had a problem when his anointing that he places on his servants is already a burden remover and yoke destroyer, as **Isaiah 10:27** states, **"it shall come to pass in that day that his burden will be taken away from your shoulder, and his yoke from your neck and the yoke will be destroyed because of the anointing oil."** If God's anointing can destroy every problem, how can we say that he has a burden that he has not been able to solve?

We have been told that God is perfect **Matthew 5:48** states, **"Therefore you shall be perfect, just as your father in heaven is perfect."** We are told that he is all-powerful and that there is nothing he cannot do, **Luke 1:37**, **"For, with God, nothing will be impossible."** The prophet Jeremiah said in **Jeremiah 51:15, "He has made the earth by his power; he has established the world by his wisdom and stretched out the heaven by his understanding."**

If all this is true of God, how can he be said to have a problem or a burden?

The truth is that God does not just have a burden, he has a nagging burden, one that gives him a headache and constitutes a major problem for him.

A problem can be defined as something difficult to deal with or understand. God in his infinite wisdom finds it very difficult to understand why anyone would not want to go to heaven but would choose hell instead. God created us to be free moral agents, we can choose to do whatever we want. Even though heaven is his desire for us, he cannot force us to go there. He tells us in **Deuteronomy 30:19 "I call heaven and earth as witnesses today**

against you, that I have set before you life and death, blessing and cursing; therefore choose life, that both you and your descendants may live." As independent creations, the choice is ours. In this scripture, however, God is telling us to choose heaven over hell.

Let us for a moment imagine what hell is like. Fire here on earth can only burn you if you move close to it, the effects of the fire are external, it burns the skin. Hell fire on the other hand burns both internally and externally; it is all-consuming and it never ends. Imagine the excruciating, constant pain that someone in hell must go through; an everlasting pain with no reprieve. Why would anyone in their right mind choose that kind of pain over the peace and comfort of heaven?

There are no problems in heaven, all the issues that we face here on earth, problems of health, finances and so forth are not present, instead, there is peace, joy, and happiness. There is no evil, no household wickedness, no attacks or discomfort of any sort. All you will hear being sung in heaven are praises and worship to the Most High God.

The Almighty God does not want any of us to go through eternal pain in hell. He loves us and his intention and plan and purpose for our lives is that we will be blessed here on earth and end up in heaven. However, our sinful nature makes it very difficult for God to do what he wants to do in our lives. He could bless us here on earth with everything that we desire, regardless of whether or not what he gives us will lead to our destruction but that would mean discarding all his plans of our making heaven.

Alternatively, he could bless us with what we want but keep us locked up in one place so that we do not sin but that will be taking away our free will. Finally, he has the option of choosing not to bless us at all, in which case unbelievers will claim that the God that we serve is not capable of blessing us. So God is faced with a dilemma as to how to deal with this issue that has been a great burden in his mind.

One of the parables that Jesus told his disciples during his ministry on earth is the parable of the great banquet which is recounted in **Matthew 22** and **Luke 14**. For this book, we shall be using the account in **Luke 14**. Before we look at **Luke 14** in detail, let's establish a point from **Matthew 22**. Here, Jesus begins the parable in verse 2 with the words, **"the kingdom of heaven is like a certain king who arranged a marriage for his son."** While this sentence is omitted from the version in Luke 14 it is important when considering the parable to bear in mind that Jesus was talking about heaven and the conditions that have to be met for those who will eventually end up in heaven.

Luke 14:16-24 "Then he said to him, A certain man gave a great supper and invited many, and sent his servant at supper time to say to those who were invited, 'come, for all things are now ready.' But they all with one accord began to make excuses. The first said to him, 'I have bought a piece of ground, and I must go and see it. I ask that you have me excused.' And another said 'I have bought five yoke of oxen, and I am going to test them, I ask you to have me excused.' Still another said, I have married a wife, and therefore I cannot come.' So that servant came and reported these things to his master. Then the master of the house, being angry, said to his servant, 'Go out quickly into the streets and lanes of the city, and bring in here the poor and the maimed and the lame and the blind'. And the servant said, 'Master, it is done as you commanded, and still there is room.' Then the master said to the servant, 'Go out into the highways and hedges and compel them to come in, that my house may be filled. 'For I say to you that none of those men who were invited shall taste my supper".

The man who was throwing the wedding banquet had sent out invitations to certain special people that he expected to entertain at the banquet. On the day of the banquet, however, these people turned down the invitation and give a variety of excuses for not being able to attend. At the end of the day, it was the people you would not expect to see at such a banquet who were the ultimate beneficiaries of all that had been prepared.

From this parable, it is clear to see the great burden of the Most High God. He has prepared a place for all of us in heaven as Jesus declared in **John 14:2 "In My Father's house are many mansions; if it were not so, I would have told you. I go to prepare a place for you."** These mansions in heaven have been prepared to be inhabited by human beings; they are intended for the righteous. However; the way that we humans have been behaving since the beginning of time has given God cause for concern as to who will end up inhabiting the many mansions that have been prepared. **Revelations 22:12** states, **"And behold, I am coming quickly, and My reward is with me, to give to every one according to his work"**. This means that when Jesus returns we will be judged and whether or not we make heaven will depend on what we have done while we were here on earth.

When God looks at our hearts and our attitudes he is concerned that none of us will make it. When he reminds us about heaven and what we need to do to ensure that we make it, instead of doing what is right and obeying his word, we keep giving him flimsy excuses, unmindful of the destruction that we are building up for ourselves. When we give these excuses, we are effectively turning down God's invitation to enter heaven, the same way that the guest turned down the invitation to attend the wedding banquet. The result will be as is stated, in **Luke 22:23-24**, those of us who God had prepared those mansions for will never live in them, while people who did not consider themselves worthy will eventually inhabit them.

We have established that one of the major problems that God is dealing with is man and our unwillingness to do what it takes so that we will make heaven. This is not the only problem that God has ever encountered. Let us look in the bible to identify some of the other issues that have confronted God in the past and see how he dealt with them.

Our first example is taken from **Genesis 1:1-3** which states, **"In the beginning, God created the heavens and the earth. The earth was without form and void, and darkness was on the face of the deep. And the spirit of God was hovering over the face of the waters. Then God said, "Let there be light" and there was light"**.

The problem that God faced at the beginning of time was darkness and emptiness, no one likes darkness and emptiness because very little can be achieved where both are present. God however solved the problems with his anointing through his word. He decreed light, it came to pass and he was then able to accomplish all that he wanted to.

The second example is taken from **Exodus 14** when the children of Israel were fleeing from the oppression of the Egyptians. The lord had worked mighty miracles in Egypt to compel Pharaoh to let the children of Israel go but on their way to the Promised Land, they encountered the red sea. In addition to this, the Egyptians were chasing after them so they had nowhere to turn. How did God solve this seemingly insurmountable problem? In **Exodus 14: 15-16** we read **"And the LORD said to Moses, "why do you cry to me? Tell the children of Israel to go forward. "But lift up your rod, and stretch out your hand over the sea and divide it. And the children of Israel shall go on dry ground through the midst of the sea".** God told Moses to part the red sea and the red sea parted. The supposedly difficult problem was solved instantly and no longer represented a problem to God.

The third example is taken from the Book of Joshua. Joshua had a battle to fight on behalf of the Lord and even though he was winning the battle, time was against him. He knew that if night fell, some of his enemies would escape and that if they escaped they would certainly rally and return to fight him. God solved the problem by stopping the passage of time and halting the setting of the sun and the rising of the moon. **Joshua 10:12-13** states, **"Then Joshua spoke to the LORD in the day when the Lord delivered up the Amorites before the children of Israel, and he said in the sight of Israel: "Sun, stand still over Gibeon; and Moon, in the valley of Aijalon." So the sun stood still, and the moon stopped, till the people had revenge upon their enemies. Is this not written in the book of Jasher? So the sun stood still in the midst of heaven, and did not hasten to go down for about a whole day."**

From these examples, we can see that generally, God does not have a problem with things that he has created. If anything seems to be presenting an obstacle to him, he simply commands it to do his will and it obeys. So why does man present such a persistent problem to God? You could argue that the examples we looked at where God commanded darkness to become light, the red sea to part and the sun and the moon to stop dealt with nature and that problem began to arise when dealing with reasoning creations. However, in **Matthew 6** when Jesus is teaching his disciples how to pray he says in verse 10 **"Your kingdom come. Your will be done on earth as it is in heaven".** This tells us that God has no problem in heaven because the angels are doing his will. Even Satan and his hosts do not present a persistent problem to God because he simply created hell for them, threw them into it and commanded them to stay there. Satan cannot go into heaven and try to overthrow God.

Man was created in God's image and endowed with intelligence and free will. God loved man so much that he blessed him abundantly, giving him incredible power and authority and everything else that he would need to be successful in life. Having given man so much, you would expect that man would be grateful to God and that he would not present a problem to him. Unfortunately, this is not the case. From the time that God created man, man has presented himself as a burden to God and has turned down God's invitation to enter heaven.

The burden that man has presented to God is a three-stage burden, two of which are in the past while the third stage is an ongoing burden. For this book, I will refer to the first stage as "the great burden of God" , the second stage as "the greater burden of God" and the final current stage as "the greatest burden of God".

The great burden of God refers to the early man, God's first creation before the flood that destroyed the world. This first burden is represented by the man in **Luke 14:18** who gave as his excuse for not attending the wedding banquet the fact that he had just bought a field and had to go look at it. The greater burden of God refers to the children of Israel, the descendants of Abraham who God chose as his special people. They are represented by the guest in **Luke 14:19** who said that he had just bought some oxen and needed to test them. The third burden of God refers to present-day man, which you and I are a part of and they are represented by the man in **Luke 14:20** who stated that he had just married a wife and could not, therefore, attend the feast. Over the next few chapters, we shall be looking in detail at each of these groups of people and examining in what way they constituted a burden to God and turned down his invitation to enter heaven.

Chapter 2

THE GREAT BURDEN OF GOD

The first of the three groups of men that turned God down is early man, a group I refer to as the great burden of God. God had high hopes for man when he created him. He made man in His likeness and gave him power over the whole world. In **Genesis 1:26** God said, **"Let Us make man in Our image, according to Our likeness; let them have dominion over the fish of the sea, over the birds of the air, and over the cattle, over all the earth and over every creeping thing that creeps on the earth."** God ordered man in **Genesis 1:28** to **"be fruitful and multiply; fill the earth and subdue it."** The earth and everything in it were created to be under man's control and for his sustenance and pleasure.

If you remember the parable of the wedding banquet in **Luke 14** that we looked at in Chapter One, the first man who rejected the invitation to the banquet gave as his excuse the fact that he had just bought a piece of land and needed to look at it. You could liken this man to the early man who had been given the whole earth and all that was in it for his pleasure but despite this, he chose to reject God. All that man had to do was enjoy what God had created for him and express his gratitude and love to his creator. Man, however, had other ideas. **Ecclesiastes 7:29** states, **"Truly, this only I have found: that God made man upright, but they have sought out many schemes."**

God created man in his image, without any imperfection or corruption but man turned away from his maker and looked for different ways of fulfilment. The things that man turned to were full of evil and wickedness. **Genesis 6:5** states, **"Then the Lord saw that the wickedness of man was great in the earth and that every**

intent of the thoughts of his heart was only evil continually." Evil dominated the heart of man. **Matthew 15:19** states, **"For out of the heart proceed evil thoughts, murders, adulteries, fornications, thefts, false witness, blasphemies."** Rather than remaining in the image of God who is perfect, man became the epitome of corruption itself, and could only do evil. **In Genesis 6:3** God noted that man is "flesh" and that as a result, his spirit, **"would not strive with him forever,"** It is the Holy Spirit working within man that allows him to conform to the image of God. However, when man resists the Holy Spirit and persists in fulfilling the lusts and desires of his flesh, then the Holy Spirit can no longer operate within man.

Over time evil ultimately came to rule over early man and there was no redeeming feature in him whatsoever. The evil that man did was not out of ignorance or carelessness but was done with willful and determined intent. Every thought that man had, came from evil; his ideas and perceptions all sprang from evil and as a result, all man's purposes, wishes, desires and motives were evil. No matter how innocent his actions may have seemed on the surface, evil was the driving force behind them. This evil was all over the earth and as is stated in **Genesis 6:11**, the whole earth **"was corrupt before God, and the earth was filled with violence."**

The phrase, "corrupt before God" means that early man had either placed other gods before the Most High God or had abandoned their worship and reverence of him totally and were boldly defiant in their disobedience and scorn of his ways. Violence and injustice were the order of the day and as there was no government to put in place regulations and to police the actions of the people, havoc and mayhem reigned supreme. There was no trace of righteousness amongst men with each seeking to devour the other, without any sense of justice or propriety. This shows us that without the fear of God, man is reduced to the savagery that is comparable to the behaviour of wild beasts in the jungle.

This state of affairs was far from what God had intended when he created man. **Genesis 6:6** states, **"And the Lord was sorry that he had made man on the earth and he was grieved in his heart."** The New Living Translation of the Bible translates this verse as **"So, the Lord was sorry he had ever made them. It broke his heart."** Can you imagine what it is for the Almighty God to feel heartbroken? And to think that the cause of God's heartbreak was man who he had done so much for!

Imagine that you have been kind to someone, worked very hard to provide for them and give them everything that they desire and after you have done all this, the person turns around and betrays you. How would you feel? Undoubtedly you would wish that you had never met the person and had not wasted all your time and energy trying to please him. You would wish that you could turn back time to erase everything that you ever did for him. There is a real-life story that I will use here to illustrate my point.

A woman who had a grade three teaching certificate got married to a man who had the same educational qualification as she did. This woman was the only child of a widow who had worked hard all her life to make enough money to send her daughter to university. Upon her marriage, however, the woman told her mother that she no longer wanted to go to university. She begged her mother to use the money she had saved to send her husband to university instead of her. She reasoned that the bible says that the man is supposed to be the head of the family and so it would not be right if she went to university, and got a higher educational qualification than her husband. She believed that such a situation would cause problems in her home and felt that if her husband went to university and did well in life, then it would also be good for her. Her mother agreed and used her hard-earned money to send her son-in-law to university.

After graduating, the husband got a good, well-paid job and began to do very well in life. He got promotion after promotion until he was a high powered executive. It was at this point that he began to look down on his wife. He forgot where he was coming from and decided that someone with his wife's low level of education was not the right sort of wife that a successful man like him should have. He was ashamed of her because he felt that she was not sophisticated and could not mix or fit in with the type of people that he had to associate with at his level. He felt that she would disgrace him and so he proceeded to discard her and marry another wife he felt would suit his lifestyle better. The woman who had abandoned her education for this man and convinced her mother to squander her fortune on him was completely heartbroken and became a mental wreck.

The betrayal that this woman suffered at the hands of her husband is nothing when you compare it to what God experienced with early man. We know that God worked for six days to create the earth. He took his time to prepare a wonderful place for man to live in and gave man everything that he could desire so that he could have a good life. Instead of showing love and gratitude to God, however, man rejected all that God had offered him and turned his back on him, choosing instead to follow a sinful path. Sin is anathema to God; He despises it and cannot abide it. It is therefore no surprise that he was grieved to the heart by man's behaviour. **Psalms 5:4** states of God, "**For you are not a God who takes pleasure in wickedness, nor shall evil dwell with you.**" **Psalm 11:5-7** states further, **"The Lord tests the righteous, but the wicked and the one who loves violence his soul hates. Upon the wicked he will rain coals; fire and brimstone and a burning wind shall be the portion of their cup. For the Lord is righteous, He loves righteousness; His countenance beholds the upright."**

From these verses, it is clear that whatever is sinful cannot abide by God. God created man for his pleasure but he could take no pleasure in man when all that was in him was wickedness and when as is stated in **Genesis 6:5, "every intent of the thoughts of his heart was only evil continually."**

Because of the evil that dwelt within man, God's heart turned away from him. **Genesis 6:7** states, "**So the Lord said "I will destroy man whom I have created from the face of the earth, both man and beast, creeping things and birds of the air, for I am sorry that I have made them.**" The King James Version of the Bible translates the second half of this verse as, **"for it repenteth me that I have made them."** When we read these words, we should not think that it means that God changed his mind toward man. We know that according to **Numbers 23:19, "God is not a man that He should lie nor a son of man, that he should repent. Has he said, and will he not do? Or has He spoken, and will He not make it good?"** It was not God that changed but man. God created man to be righteous because man was created in God's image and God is righteousness. When Good first made man, He was pleased with him and this showed in his dealings with man. However, when man changed and turned to iniquity, God's ways toward man also had to change.

God had a general solution to the general sinfulness of the generality of man and this solution was total destruction. He resolved to destroy not only man but also all the animals that were on earth because they were made for man. It was as if God wanted to wipe away any trace of man and everything that had been created for him from the face of the earth. The only ones who were to be spared were Noah and his family because as we are told in **Genesis 6:8**, "**Noah found grace in the eyes of the Lord.**"

The fact that God resolved to destroy every living being on earth apart from Noah says a great deal about the type of man that Noah was. **Genesis 6:9** states, "**Noah was a just man, perfect in his generations. Noah walked with God.**" Out of all the people that were on the earth, only Noah and his family were singled out for salvation. Noah found grace in the eyes of the lord because of the difference between him and all of the rest of mankind. While other men were wicked and corrupt, Noah was described as "**a just man, perfect in his generations. (Genesis 6:9)** While other men were filled with violence and harboured evil in their hearts, Noah walked with God. The point is that God did not just randomly pick Noah to be saved. He says in **Jeremiah 17:10** "**I the LORD, search the heart, I test the mind, even to give every man according to his ways, according to the fruit of his doings.**" God searched the hearts and characters of every single man on earth and only Noah was found to be worthy; all the others were only good enough for destruction.

Hebrews 11:7 states, "**By faith Noah, being warned of God of things not seen as yet, moved with fear, prepared an ark to the saving of his house; by the which he condemned the world, and became heir of the righteousness which is by faith.**"

When God told Noah what his intentions toward mankind were and instructed him to build the ark, Noah exhibited the reverence and fear that he had for God by obeying him. By putting complete belief in the words of God, acting in faith and not allowing the circumstances or the reaction of the people around him to sway him from his course, he showed why he alone amongst all men had been singled out for salvation. His actions condemned the men around him even more because of the marked contrast between his righteousness and the wickedness of their ways.

It was not difficult for God to destroy mankind. **Genesis 7:11-12** describes it as follows. "**In the six hundredth year of Noah's life, in the second month, the seventeenth day of the month, on that day all the fountains of the great deep were broken up, and the windows of heaven were opened. And the rain was on the earth forty days and forty nights.**" All it took for God to wipe off the wicked from the earth was to cause water to come up from the sea and also to pour down from the heavens. This shows us how easily God can wipe away anything that is a burden to him. It will not cost him anything to do it and that is why I feel sorry for people who think that they are doing God a favour by worshipping him. We cannot do without God but He can certainly do without us. Jesus says in **Luke 3:8** that God can raise children of Abraham from mere stones so we should not think more of ourselves than we ought to.

Destruction is the end that awaits the wicked and anyone who turns their back on God. A special place has been created for those who reject God's invitation to enjoy eternal life in heaven. **Psalm 9:17** states, **"The wicked shall be turned into hell, and all the nations that forget God."** Early man in his wickedness was turned to hell and for the most part, we know who can be classified as wicked; murderers, thieves, fraudsters, fornications, adulterers, homosexuals and so on. This verse tells us, however, that in addition to those who are openly wicked and irreverent, some other less obvious candidates will also share the same fate as the wicked. Those who are unmindful of God and do not acknowledge him in their ways and their works, those who do not have any regard for God's teachings and do not believe in him, no matter how honest, kind, generous or upright they may seem to be, will also be turned to hell.

Given the foregoing, can you honestly say that you are a candidate of heaven or will you join the wicked and those who have forgotten God in hell? When we look at the description of hell, it is a place of everlasting sorrow.

Revelations 20:10 describes it as **"the lake of fire and brimstone where the beast and the false prophet are. And they will be tormented day and night forever and ever."**

When a man is turned into hell, who would want to associate with him or have anything to do with him? Hell is a place where nothing good can happen so who in their right mind would want their lives turned into hell?

Our time on this earth is very short. Our lives go by in the blink of an eye and every day we are moving closer and closer to the moment when we will bid this world goodbye. Every soon, all the things that we are chasing after that cause us to turn our back on God and ignore him will become meaningless. God has prepared a place for us to enjoy in heaven but so many of us are showing him by our actions that we are not candidates for heaven that he is left to wonder exactly who will occupy the many mansions He has prepared for his children. Despite the shortage of qualified candidates, however, God will never compromise his standards to suit us. We must fulfil all the requirements if we are to make heaven.

The pursuit of anything to the detriment of God is futile because one day, all these things will pass away. Only God sticks with you through the thick and thin of your life; only he can be counted upon to be with you in trial and tribulation, in your sickness, in your sadness, in your sorrow and your despairs. He is a very present help and will never leave you or forsake you. That same God is telling you that he has prepared a place of eternal rest for you and is inviting you to come and fellowship with him there.

What is your response to his invitation?

The wickedness of early man and the widespread evil that was on the earth caused God to destroy the whole of mankind. Man had become a burden to God and so he removed them from the face of the earth except for Noah and his children. God believed that once he wiped away his great burden, early man, and started anew with Noah and his generations then the problem of man would be solved once and for all. If we look around us now, however, can we say that anything has changed? The earth is still full of wickedness and the evil that was in the heart of early man can also be found in the hearts of men today.

So what went wrong? The solution that God introduced to deal with the problem of the great burden of early man, simply resulted in an even greater burden. We shall be looking at this greater burden in the next chapter.

Chapter 3

THE GREATER BURDEN OF GOD

As we stated in the previous chapter, the great burden of God was early man. His wickedness and the evil of his heart caused God to wipe him away from the face of the earth and to start afresh with Noah and his children. **Genesis 9:1** states, **"So God blessed Noah and his sons, and said to them: "Be fruitful, multiply, and fill the earth".**

Out of Noah's descendants, God chose Abraham with whom to establish his covenant. In **Genesis 12:2-3**, God said to Abraham, **"I will make you a great nation; I will bless you and make your name great; and you shall be a blessing. I will bless those who bless you, and I will curse him who curses you; and in you, all the families of the earth shall be blessed."**

It was because of the special relationship that God had with Abraham that his descendants, the children of Israel, were chosen and loved above all other people on the earth. **Exodus 19:6** states, **"And you shall be to me a kingdom of priest and a holy nation,"** and **Deuteronomy 7:6** reaffirms, **"For you are a holy people to the LORD your God; the LORD your God has chosen you to be a people for Himself, a special treasure above all the peoples on the face of the earth.**

The children of Israel were variously described in the bible as a peculiar people, a peculiar treasure, a holy nation, a special people; a kingdom of priests, set apart from the rest of mankind to the service of God and the execution of his divine purpose. They were chosen as God's beloved people to show forth his righteousness so that other nations would look at them, at the righteousness of their lives, at their devotion to and special relationship with God and learn from their example. They were not chosen because there were more of them than other people on the earth or because they were particularly worthy, but simply as a result of God's special relationship with their ancestors.

1 Corinthians 10:26 Tells us that the earth is the Lord's and all its fullness. As God's special treasure, the children of Israel would have had access to everything that was the Lord's. In **Deuteronomy 28:1-14**, the Lord described to the children of Israel all the blessings that would come upon them if they were obedient, harkened to his voice and did not turn away from him to serve other gods. **Deuteronomy 28:1** states, **"Now it shall come to pass, if you diligently obey the voice of the LORD your God, to observe carefully all his commandments which I command you today, that the LORD your God will set you high above all nations of the earth."** The blessings that were promised to the children of Israel are numerous and they included safety and security wherever they went, fruitfulness, abundance, success, honour amongst their neighbours and victory over their enemies.

The children of Israel were indeed blessed and highly favoured by the lord but it was this blessing that led them to become a greater burden of God than early man had been. Every time the Lord smiled upon the children of Israel and blessed them, they would sin. In the parable in **Luke 14**, which we looked at in chapter one, the second invited guest to the wedding banquet who refused the invitation gave the following excuse **"I have bought five yoke of oxen, and I am going to test them. I ask you to have me excused' (Luke 14:19)**. It was the blessings that the Lord had showered upon the guest that led to the excuse he gave for not attending the wedding banquet. If he had not been blessed with the wherewithal to buy the oxen, then he would not have had any excuse for not attending the banquet. In the same way, if the Lord had not blessed the children of Israel, then the opportunity for sin would not have presented itself.

The children of Israel provoked God with their behaviour. He said of them in **Isaiah 65:2-3, "I have stretched out my hands all day long to a rebellious people who walk in a way that is not good, according to their own thoughts; a people who provoke me to anger continually to my face."** They defied His authority, refused to conform to his rules and turned away from him to worship other Gods. As we saw in **Deuteronomy 28:1**, the Lord laid down his commandments and expected the children of Israel to abide by them. The adherence to these commandments was the condition for the blessings that he showered upon them. However, the children of Israel had great difficulty following these commandments because, by nature, they were a rebellious people.

It is easy for us to look at the children of Israel and condemn them for their rebellious behaviour but many children of God today are exhibiting the same attitudes towards God. If your servant of God has ever given you information from the Holy Spirit about what God expects you to do and you go ahead and do what you want to do anyway, then you are no different from the children of Israel. Every time you hear the word of God or receive instructions from him but still follow your head knowledge then you are provoking God to his face just like the Israelites did. You may think that you are only disobeying the servant of God but you are defying God in the same way that the children of Israel defied him when they murmured against the instructions that Moses had passed on to them from God.

In **Deuteronomy 9:7**, Moses reminded the children of Israel about their behaviour when he told them, **"Remember! Do not forget how you provoked the LORD your God to wrath in the wilderness. From the day that you departed from the land of Egypt until you came to this place, you have been rebellious against the LORD"** The long journey through the wilderness was one of constant murmuring, grumbling and rebelling against the Most High God. It was only through Moses' prayers of intercession that God did not destroy them as he had destroyed the early man before them. Moses had to plead with the Lord to spare their lives.

Exodus 32:11-14 "Then Moses pleaded with the LORD his God, and said: "LORD, why does your wrath burn hot against your people whom you have brought out of the land of Egypt with great power and with a mighty hand? Why should the Egyptians speak, and say, 'He brought them out to harm them, to kill them in the mountains, and to consume them from the face of the earth? Turn from your fierce wrath, and relent from this harm to your

people. Remember Abraham, Isaac and Israel, your servants to whom you swore by yourself, and said to them, 'I will multiply your descendants as the stars of heaven; and all this land that I have spoken of I give to your descendants, and they shall inherit it forever.' So the Lord relented from the harm which he said he would do to his people."

In the same way, I sometimes have to plead with the Lord to have mercy upon some of my spiritual sons and daughters when they go against the Lord's specific instructions for their lives.

The bible gives us numerous instances of the children of Israel failing to do what is expected of them, despite the blessings that God had showered upon them. We shall look at Eli and Saul, whose lives are a prime example of why the children of Israel became the greater burden of God.

Eli was a descendant of Aaron to whose descendants the priesthood had been granted for perpetuity. Eli was the high priest of Israel at the time when Samuel was a child. By then he was very old and his two sons Hophni and Phinehas had taken over a lot of the priestly duties. We are told in **1 Samuel 2:12** that, **"the sons of Eli were corrupt; they did not know the lord."** The King James version of the bible translates that verse as, **"The sons of Eli were sons of Belial."** The sons of Belial are the devils' children, perverse and wicked with pure evil in their hearts. Hophni and Phinehas committed numerous atrocious acts and their actions as priests were directly responsible for the ungodliness that was prevalent amongst the children of Israel at the time **1 Samuel 2:17** states, **"Therefore the sin of the young men was very great before the Lord, for men abhorred the offering of the lord."** When the Israelites saw that their priests who were supposed to set an example of righteousness for them were covetous and dissolute and engaged in all manner of lewd and unholy acts, they turned their backs on the Most High God.

Instead of Eli dealing with his son's iniquity by stripping them of their priesthood and casting them out of the temple, he merely scolded them lightly, as if the acts they had committed were not that serious. He had the power and the authority to deal with the problem if he wanted to but by keeping them in their positions, and indulging his sons' atrocious behaviour, he was an implicit accomplice to their actions.

Since Eli did not deal with the problem to his satisfaction, God decided to step into the situation and handle it himself. He said to Eli in **1 Samuel 2:29-30 'Why do you kick at my sacrifice and my offering which I have commanded in my dwelling place, and honour our sons more than me, to make yourselves fat with the best of all the offerings of Israel my people?' "Therefore the LORD God of Israel says: 'I said indeed that your house and the house of our father would walk before me forever.' But now the LORD says: 'Far be it from Me; for those who honour me I will honour, and those who despise Me shall be lightly esteemed."**

God removed Eli and the whole of his family from the priesthood and in one fell swoop, all their power and influence was removed. God stated that their sins would never be forgiven and also pronounced a curse upon them so that they would all die young.

Eli's sin was that he put his sons before God who was described in **Deuteronomy 4:24** as a jealous God. By allowing his sons to take a portion of the sacrifices before they were properly offered unto the Lord, Eli showed that he honoured his sons above God. It is a great sin for parents to place their children above God in their hearts. Children are blessings that are given to us from the Most High God and as with all things that we receive from God, we should never allow them to take us away from his presence. If we do so, then we are opening ourselves up to the type of punishment that Eli and his family received.

Many of us choose to say that we serve a merciful and kind God but we tend to forget that we also serve a jealous God, who has the power of life and death in his hands. Because we believe that the God we serve is a merciful God who will forgive us our sins, we tend to be complacent about dealing with the issues in our lives that we know are contrary to the word of God. We conveniently forget that the Most High God chooses whom he will forgive. As **Romans 9:15** states, **"I will have mercy on whomever I will have mercy, and I will have compassion on whomever I will have compassion."** God can choose to be merciful to us but he can also suddenly decide not to have mercy on us any longer. He is still the same God who resolved never to forgive Eli and his descendants so we should be careful not to take his mercy for granted.

Another example of a child of Israel who became a burden to God is Saul. At one point in time the nation of Israel cried out to God to appoint a king over them and so God chose Saul to be anointed as king of Israel. At the time that God chose Saul, he was not a man of consequence, he was a nobody with only his good looks and great height to set him apart from the average person. So low was he even in his estimation that when Samuel told him that he had been chosen to be king, Saul replied in **1 Samuel 9:21 "Am I not a Benjamite, of the smallest of the tribe of Israel, and my family the least of all the families of the tribe of Benjamin? Why then do you speak like this to me?"**

In the first days after he had been anointed, Saul's respect for Samuel can be seen in the way that he obeyed every instruction the priest gave to him. After he had been king for some time, however, Saul started to go against the instructions that the Lord gave him through Samuel and began to take the law into his own hands. The first thing that he did was to offer the burnt offering and peace sacrifices to the Lord instead of waiting for Samuel to do it as was the normal practice. Saul had no authority to offer any sacrifices to the lord but he ignored this fact and did as he pleased. As a result of this act, the Lord's heart was turned against Saul. Samuel told him in **1 Samuel 13:13-14, "You have done foolishly. You have not kept the commandment of the Lord your God, which he commanded you. For now, the LORD would have established your kingdom over Israel forever. But now your kingdom shall not continue."**

We are not told in the bible that Saul apologised or showed any remorse and so we can assume that he did not feel that he had done anything wrong. This view is supported by Saul's actions, in **1 Samuel 15** when he went against the instructions that Samuel had given him to destroy Amalek and everything in it, including all the livestock. Rather than obeying fully, Saul kept the best of the livestock for himself and his men and also spared the life of Agag the king of the Amalekites.

When Samuel confronted him with this latest disobedience, Saul again showed no remorse and tried to justify his actions, by saying that he took some of the livestock to sacrifice to God. Samuel responded to him in **1 Samuel 15:22-23 "Has the LORD as great delight in burnt offerings and sacrifices, as in obeying the voice of the LORD? Behold, to obey is better than sacrifice, and to heed than the fat of rams. For rebellion is as the sin of witchcraft, and stubbornness is as iniquity and idolatry. Because you have rejected the word of the lord, he also has rejected you from being king".** Disobedience to God's commandments cannot simply be assuaged with sacrifice as Saul believed. The result of his constant and persistent disobedience was that God rejected him as a king.

God did not have any problems with Saul until He anointed him as king but once he had been blessed, Saul allowed the blessings to get to his head. In the same way, nowadays when God blesses his children, it is those same blessings that cause them to move away from his presence. A lot of people are no longer managing their blessings; it is their blessings that are managing them. They fail to remember that we did not bring anything into this world and we will not take anything with us when we leave it.

The accounts of Eli and Saul that we find in the Bible are representative of the lives of the generality of the children of Israel. They were a rebellious people and time again they disregarded the instructions of the Lord and did things to provoke him to anger like Saul. They were also adulterous in that they frequently turned away from him to serve other gods or placed other things above him like Eli. The result was that the Lord sold them to their enemies.

In **Ezra 9:7** the priest Ezra says of his people the children of Israel, **"Since the days of our fathers, to this day we have been very guilty, and for our iniquities we, our kings and our priests have been delivered into the hand of the kings of the lands, to the sword, to captivity, to plunder, and to humiliation, as it is this day."**

Do you provoke God with your actions and your thoughts? Those who provoke God are not going to heaven but will end up in eternal hell fire. They will be rejected just as the children of Israel, who constituted the greater burden of God were rejected by him.

Chapter 4

THE GREATEST BURDEN OF GOD

The third group of people who are the greatest burden of god are not terrorists, murders or assassins as one world expect they are not the atheists who boldly say that there is no God, nor are they those who prosecute and murder Christians. These groups of people are not problems for God because they are not part of him, they do not factor into the equation and are of no consequence. He already has a place prepared for them in eternal hell fire.

It may surprise you to learn that God's greatest burden is the church. After both early man and the children of Israel had failed him, God decided to do something different. He sent his only begotten son, Jesus intending to establish a church, a body of believers consecrated onto him. He believed that with the church, he could prepare for himself a group of people who would be qualified to make heaven and who would inhabit the many mansions that he had prepared. You may recall that we said earlier that the issue of who would make heaven was the reason that God destroyed the early man. The early man was too wicked and evil to inhabit the mansions in heaven and so God resolved the start again with the children of Israel. They, however, proved to be a disappointment because of their rebellious and faithless nature. God then decided to send Jesus, not for the sake of the children of Israel, but for the sake of the church, the family of believers.

The bible describes the church as **"the body of Christ" (Romans 12:5)**. It is made up of Christians, the group of people who believe that Jesus Christ is their Lord and saviour and that through him they can gain eternal life. **Ephesians 1:22-23** states, **"And he put all things under his feet, and gave him to be head over all things to**

the church, which is his body, the fullness of him who fills all in all." Through Jesus Christ, its head, the body of Christ is filled with all spiritual gifts and graces and empowered to accomplish mighty things for God here on earth.

The church can also be defined as an aggregation of those who are segregated from the world. They are in this world but they are no longer of this world. Jesus said to God of his disciples and therefore by extension of every member of the body of Christ **"I have manifested your name to the men whom you have given me out of the world. They were yours, you gave them to me, and they have kept your word." (John 17:6).** This means that once we become members of the body of Christ, we are called out of the world unto Christ. Our physical bodies may still be in this world, but we are not supposed to conform to the behaviour of this world.

The body of Christ has been separated from the rest of mankind, much as the children of Israel had been in the past. In **1 Peter 2:9**, Christians are even described using the same terms that were used to describe the Israelites in the Old Testament. **"But you are a chosen generation, a royal priesthood, a holy nation, His own special people, that you may proclaim the praises of him who called you out of darkness into his marvellous light."**

The reason that members of the body of Christ have been granted these privileges is so that they may show forth the goodness and perfection of God. We are meant to live holy and useful lives, being transformed into the image of God, walking in Christ's footsteps and following his commandments. **Romans 12:2** states, **"And do not be conformed to this world, but be transformed by the renewing of your mind that you may prove what is that good and acceptable and perfect will of God."**

The body of Christ should not conform to the ways of this world because as stated in **1 John 5:19, "We know that we are of God, and the whole world lies under the sway of the wicked one."** Jesus Christ died to **"deliver us from this present evil age" (Galatians 1:4)** and so if we are truly his followers then we must reject everything that the world stands for and not walk according to the flesh but according to the spirit **(Roman 8:4)**.

Nowadays, however, a lot of people who profess to be Christians are still in the world. If you compare them to someone who is not a Christian, you would not be able to see any differences. They dress the same, talk the same and exhibit the same attitudes as those who are in the world. Every decision that they take is based on the world system and not on the word of God. They forget that as Christians, they are not supposed to emulate the world, rather the world is supposed to look at them and see that it is possible to live a righteous life. Worldly Christians want to blend with the world and are afraid of being tagged as radicals. They do not want to go through the same suffering that Christ experienced while he was here on earth yet they want to enjoy his anointing.

What is the role of the church here on earth? Jesus described it in **Matthew 5:13-16 "You are the salt of the Earth; but if the salt loses its flavour, how shall it be seasoned? It is then good for nothing but to be thrown out and trampled underfoot by men. You are the light of the world. A city that is set on a hill cannot be hidden. Nor do they light a lamp and put it under a basket, but on a lamp stand and it gives light to all who are in the house. Let your light so shine before men, that they may see your good works and glorify your Father in heaven."** Children of God are meant to lead others by the way they live their lives, by their words and their actions. They are meant to have a transforming effect on the world much as salt has a transforming effect over food and the light of their lives is supposed to shine so bring that it banishes all the darkness around them.

The church is meant to be a body of prefects, much like the prefects that you find in schools. Such people are supposed to be perfect and Jesus tells us in **Matthew 5:48 "Therefore you shall be perfect, just as your father in heaven is perfect."** We should be people who are walking in holiness, striving towards perfection and aiming to inhabit these mansions in heaven that the Lord has prepared for us. A prefect leads and gives instructions for others to follow and as children of God, this is what we are expected to do. Instead of leading the world, however, Christians today have become followers of the world.

The people who God called and set apart to be in charge are no longer in charge and as a result, have become a burden to God. When he looks at the church, God despairs it because it is not what he created it to be. The majority of people who call themselves Christians today and who are supposed to be members of the body of Christ do not qualify to inhabit the mansions that the Lord has prepared for them in heaven. It pains me to say that the church in its present state has failed God.

In the bible, God laid down laws that his children are meant to be following but most Christians are now following their own rules and the rules of the world. There is a very wide gap between where God expects us to be and where we are in our attitudes, our mode of dressing, the way we talk and so forth. Most people still do not understand that we have been created for God's pleasure. We were specifically made to please God but most of the time we act to please ourselves and when we do this, we displease God. We put ourselves first and consider our convenience before we think about what God expects from us. God is not interested in what is convenient for us; when he makes a demand of us, he expects us to obey immediately, not when we feel like obeying. When we honour our desires over God's then we become a burden to him.

Imagine that you employed a servant to work for you but whenever you need him to carry out the tasks for which he was employed, he gives you an excuse as to why he is not able to do his work. You may give the servant the benefit of the doubt once or twice but if his behaviour persists, you would most likely terminate his employment. Some people would not even tolerate one transgression, they would fire the servant immediately. Consider then how God must feel every time you give him an excuse for not being able to do what he has called you to do. You may feel that the excuses are legitimate but there is no excuse that you could give for not doing God's work.

When you divide the church into two, there are leaders and followers. The leaders are supposed to guide the congregation and teach them according to the word of God. What you find in most churches nowadays, however, is the blind leading the blind. **Mathew 15:14 "let them alone. They are blind leaders of the blind. And if the blind leads the blind, both will fall into a ditch,"** Ministers of God have been blinded by ambition, blinded by pride and blinded by arrogance. It is no longer about God's church but about their church. They forget that the church has nothing to do with them and that if they die tomorrow, the church will continue. The church is not a family business it is God's business, it is not about man, it is all about God.

Titus 1:7-9 spells out the qualities that a man of God should have. He should be **"blameless, as a steward of God, not self-willed, not quick-tempered, not given to wine, not silent, not greedy for money, but hospitable, a lover of what is good, sober-minded, just, holy, self-controlled, holding fast the faithful word as he had been taught."** How many servants of God can this be said of today?

A man of God once came to see me for counselling. He told me that whenever he prayed for the members of his congregation they would be blessed; they were buying cars and houses but nothing was happening in his own life and so he got angry, refused to pray for them any longer and closed down the church. I told him that he had made a big mistake. His envy of the spiritual children that God had given him turned what was supposed to be his testimony into a curse on his life. The fact that he closed down the church would not cause God to abandon his true children rather God would just direct the blessings that he purposed for them through another vessel. That he was able to so easily abandon his spiritual children because of envy and jealousy was an indicator of the wickedness of his heart and showed why God had not blessed him in the first place.

Many men of God are like this man, they believe that when they pray and something happens, it is because of their anointing. They forget that the anointing is borrowed and that it was given to them for a specific purpose. If they fall to call out that purpose to the satisfaction of God, or if they begin to think too much of themselves and their abilities, then God will take the anointing away from them and give it to someone else who is more worthy.

Ambition has caused a lot of men of God to forget what they have been called to do. They want their churches to grow and are prepared to do whatever it takes to achieve this growth. They assess their success in terms of the number of people they have in their congregation and not in terms of the holiness of the lives of the people that they are leading. What use is it to have one million members in your church if only five of them are qualified to make heaven? They have turned the churches in their care into their business and it has become all about personal achievement, it is no longer about God but about money. They love money so much that when they preach, they watch their words very carefully so that they will not offend any members of their congregation, especially those who are wealthy. They are afraid that if they offend someone, the person may leave and take their big offerings and tithes along with them. They allow their love of money to dictate what they say to their congregation in contravention of the word of God which tells servants of God not to shepherd their flock for **"dishonest gain." (1 Peter 5:2)**

Nowadays you find servants of God competing with the members of their congregation as to who will be the best dressed. If a member of their congregation is wearing a particular pair of designer shoes or a certain type of suit then they resolve that they too must wear the same thing or something even better. They forget that as leaders, they should be setting an example for their congregation and not competing with them. As men of God, their focus should be on the things of heaven and not on the things of this world. As is stated in **1 Timothy 4:12** they should **"Be examples to the believers in word, in conduct, in love, in spirit, in faith, in purity."**

What examples are servants of God setting for their congregation today? What traits could the followers possibly exhibit if their leaders are selfish and stubborn? Today so-called servants of God are irreverent and show no respect for God. They are immoral and covetous, they are liars and covenant breakers. It is no wonder then that the body of Christ has become a burden to the Almighty God.

So many people who pass through churches end up in hell. People come to church but what do they take away from church? What lessons are being taught what examples are being set for them to follow? Even in a place where the truth is being preached, there is still a problem because people are not willing to listen to the truth. Men of God are under obligation to speak the truth to their concretion. **1 Thessalonians 2:4** states, **"But as we have been**

approved by God to be entrusted with the gospel, even so, we speak, not as pleasing men, but God who tests our hearts." If they see the members of their congregation doing something wrong and fail to correct them, then they will be held accountable to God. Nowadays, however, when someone is corrected in church, they simply leave and go to another church where the servant of God preaches what they want to hear.

In **John 3:29,** the bible compared the relationship between Christ and the church as one between a bridegroom and his bride and the parable of the ten virgins and the bridegroom in **Matthew 25:1-12** echoes this analogy. You will recall that in the parable we looked at in **Luke 14:16-24** in which the guests invited for the wedding banquet gave various excuses for not attending the banquet, the third man's excuse was, **'I have married a wife, and therefore I cannot come' (Luke 14:20).** We can compare the church to the third man because the church is the bride of Christ. Some Christians believe that as members of the bride of Christ, they automatically qualify to occupy the mansions that the Lord has prepared in heaven. They fail to recognize that the current state of the church is far from what God had envisioned when he created it and that the church as an institution has failed God, just like the children of Israel and early man did in the past.

Who then will inhabit the mansions that the Lord has prepared in heaven? Over the next few chapters, we shall be looking at the things that we must do if we want to make heaven.

Chapter 5

BE TRULY BORN AGAIN

As stated in the previous chapters, God has prepared many mansions in heaven and is looking for people to occupy them. He tried three groups of people, early man, the children of Israel and finally the church but they all failed him. They fell short of divine expectation and became a burden to the Most High God. God was then left to wonder who would end up occupying the mansions he had prepared.

Let us turn once again to the parables we looked at in **Luke 14:16-24** for an answer to the questions of who will end up making heaven. After the guests gave various excuses and turned down the invitation to the wedding banquet, the servant returned to his master with the news. **Luke 14:21-24** states, **"So that servant came and reported these things to his master. Then the master of the house, being angry, said to his servant, 'Go out quickly into the streets and lanes of the city, and bring in here the poor and the maimed and the lame and the blind.' And the servant said, 'Master, it is done as you commanded, and still there is room.' Then the master said to the servant, 'Go out into the highways and hedges and compel them to come in that my house may be filled. For I say to you that none of those men who were invited shall taste my supper."**

After the three categories of guests turned down the invitation to the wedding banquet, the mater instructed his servant to go out into the street and bring in the poor, the maimed, the lame and the blind and to bring in people from the highways and the hedges; these were labourers, the very poorest of the people in society. The master resolved that only these people, considered to be the very dregs of society, would enjoy the banquet and none of the guests could come in.

We can deduce from this that the only people who would qualify to inhabit the mansions in heaven are the poor, maimed, lame and blind. We should not infer from this that Jesus was referring to their physical condition, rather he was talking about their spiritual condition. This means that the three groups of people that failed God in the past, the early man, the children of Israel and the church are no longer criteria to make heaven. Membership in these groups will not guarantee their members entry into heaven. For example, if you are a member of a church, the criteria for making heaven will not depend on the church that you attend but on whether or not you are a real Christian.

Many people who go to church today are not Christians. Such people believe that the fact that they attend church means that they are Christian but this is not the case. A true Christian is born again. **John 3:3** states, **"Jesus answered and said to him, "Most assuredly, I say to you, unless one is born again, he cannot see the kingdom of God."** This is the first thing you must-do if you want to make heaven - you must be a born again Christian.

The word born again means different things to God than it does to man. In our context, anyone who goes to church and comes forward in front of the whole congregation to surrender their life to Jesus Christ is a born again Christian whether the person means it or not. Anyone who speaks in tongues, who is an usher or a deacon in their church, anyone who calls themselves an evangelist, pastor or bishop particularly in a Pentecostal church is automatically called a born again Christian.

What does the term "born again" mean to God? Before every human being comes into this world, they must go through natural birth. Our natural birth, the birth of our earthly bodies, is the start of our sojourn here on earth but it is also the beginning of a life of sin. **Psalms 51:5** states, **"Behold, I was brought forth in iniquity, and in sin, my mother conceived me."** Our very nature is sin and in this state, we will not be able to make it to heaven. Heaven is a place of holiness and with our sinful nature, we would never qualify to enter. In the same way that a child must go through a natural birth before he can come into this world, he must go through a spiritual birth if he is to even enter the kingdom of God. This spiritual birth is a birth from heaven when our souls are brought **"out of darkness into his marvellous light" (1 Peter 2:9).** It is the beginning of our spiritual life, when we are introduced to Jesus Christ and his teachings and when our ideology, our beliefs and our attitudes are transformed from the way of the world to the way of the kingdom of heaven.

Going by God's interpretation of what being born again means, a lot of people who call themselves born again Christians are not qualified to bear that title. If you call yourself a born again Christian but everything that you do is contrary to the teachings and instructions in the bible, then you are walking in enmity to Christ. Since you are against him and not for him, you should be called born against and not born again. If you call yourself a Christian but you are still involved in lying, stealing, fornication, adultery, slander, backbiting, gossiping and all the other things that are contrary to the word of God then you are born against.

So many so-called born again Christians, especially those who are in positions of authority are using their positions to commit atrocities. There was a particular pastor who got a member of his congregation pregnant. When the girl told him that she was pregnant he accused her of being sent by Satan to destroy his ministry and told her that she was on her own. In a panic, the girl decided to have an abortion but in the process of the operation, she died. That same pastor, who was responsible for the pregnancy and indirectly responsible for the girl's death, conducted her funeral service. He confidently stood in full view of the congregation and gave a sermon using the words of God. As far as he was concerned, nobody knew about his involvement in the girl's death and so he was safe. He forgot that God sees everything and will give him the reward he deserves.

Recently a Christian brother came to me for counselling over his broken marriage. Not too long ago, he met a pastor and became close to him. They started praying together and the pastor became a regular visitor to the brother's home. Soon after, this same pastor started sleeping with the brother's wife and was directly responsible for the breakdown of his marriage. The brother trusted the pastor because he was supposed to be a born again child of God, a servant of God but he ended up regretting ever bringing him into his home.

In these two instances, the actions of the so-called men of God show that they are born against, not born again. They had never had a divine encounter with the lord otherwise they would not have been able to do the terrible things that they did. By calling themselves born again Christians and servants of God, yet deliberately committing acts that are contrary to the word they are supposed to be imparting to their congregations, they brought the name of the Lord into reproach.

Malachi 2:7-9 provides, **"For the lips of a priest should keep knowledge, and people should seek the law from his mouth; for he is the messenger of the LORD of hosts. But you have departed from the way; you have caused many to stumble at the law. You have corrupted the covenant of Levi," says the LORD of hosts. "Therefore I also have made you contemptible and base before all the people, because you have not kept my ways."** Any leader who by their irreverent and corrupt behaviour causes a child of God to fall will be severely dealt with by the Lord.

It is not just church leaders who are to blame because even when a servant of God is preaching the truth, many Christians today do not want to hear it. I heard the story of a church in London where the pastor was constantly preaching against co-habitation before marriage. It is very common in England for a man and woman to live together outside of marriage. They justify it by saying that they are sharing their bills like rent, water and telephone and claim that they are going to get married anyway but all those are simply excuses for committing fornication. The pastor kept preaching against this practice until the members of his congregation told him to stop because they felt he had made his point.

Instead of listening to them, however, the pastor persisted because obviously, God had given him a burden concerning this issue. When he continued to preach against living together in sin, people who were involved in this sin began to leave the church. What was curious, however, was that it was the ordinary members of the congregation who left and not people in positions of authority like Deacons, Ushers and so on. All of them were involved in this sin but it was only the ordinary members who felt pressure from the pastor's preaching. The others who stayed listened to everything he was saying but they refused to change, they persisted in their sin and could boldly come into church time and time again and listen to the sermons without it affecting them at all.

What does this tell us? Many so-called born again children of God have hardened their hearts against the word of God and refuse to receive correction from him. When God wants his servant to deal with a particular issue that is prevalent in the church, he will give the servant of God a burden to preach against that issue until the matter is resolved. The servant of God has no option but to obey the leading of the Holy Spirit because if he does not, then the blood of those who have fallen will be on his hands. **Ezekiel 33:7-8 "So you, son of man: I have made you a watchman for the house of Israel; therefore you shall hear a word from my mouth and warn them for me. "When I say to the wicked, 'O wicked man, you shall surely die!' and you do not speak to warn the wicked from his ways, that wicked man shall die in his iniquity, but his blood I will require at our hand"**.

Instead of hearkening to the word of the Lord and turning away from their sin, most members of the congregation kick against what they believe is the overly hard stance of the servant of God. They begin to murmur and complain, just as the children of Israel murmured and complained in the wilderness.

The question I have for such people is this. How many of you who are parents can watch your children committing acts that will lead to their downfall and remain silent? If you warn our children once or twice about their actions and they refuse to change will you then stop talking to them about it? No, you would not. Rather, you would persist and hammer on the children until they change. You would not just give up because you love your child and do not want to see them hurt?

As **Proverbs 3:11-12** states, **"My son, do not despise the chastening of the Lord, nor detest His correction; for whom the Lord loves he corrects, just as a father the son in whom he**

delights." Many who profess to be born again Christians have forgotten that when God is silent about their sin, it means that they have become abandoned projects and no longer matter to the Lord. When God persists in correcting you, it is because he wants you to change so that you will not miss heaven.

Nowadays you cannot tell the difference between those who are in the world and those who are born again Christians. A man who is still in the world commented that it is only in Nigeria that you can find a Christian with two identities; in the church, they have one identity but when they are outside the church they have another identity. It is a shame when self-professed born again Christians can be found in the nightclubs and bars, mingling with the people of this world and engaging in all sorts of iniquity. When they are in the world they conform fully to the world, from the way they look to the words in their mouth. If you were to come across them in church, however, you would not be able to recognize them. Everything about them would have been transformed, from the way they dress to the way they talk. Such people have caused those in the world to scorn born again Christians and rather than evangelising Jesus, the way they live their lives has resulted in alienating people from the gospel. For some Christians, their issue may be their inability to let go of the pleasures of the world such as nightclubs and parties, for others it may be fighting on the street or gossiping or causing discord. Whatever it is you are doing that is causing people to look upon the body of Christ with derision then you are born against and not born again.

I have had cause to discuss the matter of appearance with many of my spiritual daughters because I am concerned about the way they dress. When they are in church their appearance is modest and pleasing to God. When they are out of the church, however, their mode of dressing is radically different from the image they project in church. They may say that God looks at their heart and not their appearance so it does not matter what they wear but God gave me a revelation that refutes this argument. God does care about the way that we look but he started looking beyond our appearance because of the wickedness of man. The fact that we are born again in our dressing and wear only modest clothes does not mean that we are born again in our hearts. People nowadays have mastered the art of looking holy outside while their hearts are full of wickedness. It is for this reason that the Lord looks at our hearts to verify who we are.

God is very particular about everything about us, from the hair on our heads to the soles of our feet. He cares about the way we talk, the way we smile, the way we walk, who our friends are, who we talk to, the work we do, he cares about our whole lives. In his word, he has given us instructions as to how to live our lives and our ability to comply with these instructions determines whether we are truly born again Christians or not. If we want to make heaven, then we will do whatever it takes, no matter how inconvenient it may be, to ensure that we are qualified to enter into the kingdom of heaven.

Chapter 6

LOOK BEYOND THE CHURCH

Making heaven is not about the church that you go to or who your servant of God is, rather it is about your relationship and your walk with God. The second thing that you must therefore do to make heaven is to look beyond the church. In this context, the church refers to your pastor, the ministers and the members of the congregation.

If you want to make heaven, you must look beyond your servant of God, beyond his faults, his shortcomings and his limitations. The only one who is perfect is Jesus Christ so you must recognize that your servant of God is not perfect and is therefore bound to make mistakes. If you look at his faults and mistakes and allow them to derail you on your journey to heaven then you will only have yourself to blame. When you go to church, you do not go to see Mr A or Mrs B; you go to seek the Most High God because you know that he can be found there. Therefore when you are in church, you should focus on God's divine presence and not on anyone else's attitude.

What Satan is seeking above anything else is to remove you from the presence of God. He knows that when he does this, you will never be able to make heaven. The first person that he may try to use to remove you from the church is your servant of God because as God's representative in the church, the servant of God is our main focus. If you do not like your servant of God, do not like the way that he talks, his character or his attitude, then you are not likely to stay in the church. Even if you try to suppress your feelings and remain in the church, you will probably not benefit much from it because your spirit will not be open to receiving anything from the servant of God. This does not mean that you must like your servant of God and all the things he says all the time. If you love every word that comes out of his mouth, there is likely to be a problem because one of the main things that a pastor is supposed to do is to instruct the congregation on the word of God. **1 Thessalonians 2:4** provides, "**But as we have been approved by God to be entrusted with the gospel, even so, we speak, not as pleasing men, but God who tests our hearts**." Your servant of God is to plainly speak what the Lord has told him and should not try to couch his words to please anyone. When he is dealing with something that concerns you, then you will most likely not like him then.

You must learn to look beyond your servant of God's character and focus instead on the substance of the word that he is preaching. Ideally, we should also be able to look at their conduct and character and emulate it. As **Hebrews 13:7** states, **"Remember those who rule over you, who have spoken the word of God to you, whose faith follow, considering the outcome of their conduct."**

Sometimes, however, this is not possible. Jesus said of the Pharisees in **Matthew 23:3 "Therefore whatever they tell you to observe, that observe and do, but do not do according to their works, for they say, and do not do."** Jesus was referring here to the teachings of the Pharisees that were following the word of God. He enjoined the people to obey the truth that the Pharisees spoke but to ignore the way that they led their lives as this did not correspond to the words that they spoke.

There will likely be something about your servant of God that you do not like but you should not focus on it. Your focus should not be on his clothes or his appearance, it should not be on his family or his personal relationships, it should not even be on his relationship with God. All these things are not your business. The only thing that should concern you is the truth in the word that he speaks to you. For as long as the words that he speaks to you are the truth, nothing else about him should be your business.

God will judge his servants, it is not our place to observe and comment upon the minutiae of their lives. **1 Chronicles 16:22** states, **"Do not touch my anointed one, and do my prophets no harm."** The Lord says that the righteousness of his servants is of him and that therefore He is the one who will judge them. In chapter three, we saw the way that the Lord dealt with Hophni and Phinehas, the two sons of Eli, on whose account the children of Israel turned away from the Lord **(1 Samuel 2).** Do not put your mouth in the middle of God's dealings with his servants because you are likely to cause problems for yourself as a result.

Whenever you see your servant of God doing wrong, do not confront him about it because he is your spiritual leader, rather you should pray for him. Recall what happened to Aaron and Miriam in **Numbers 12** when they spoke against Moses because he had married an Ethiopian woman. **Numbers 12:9** states that **"The anger of the lord as aroused against them"** and Miriam was afflicted with leprosy for seven days because she was probably the instigator of the accusations against Moses.

If your servant of God is doing something you think is wrong, pray for him and close your eyes as if you cannot see the wrong that he has done. We have an example of his in **Genesis 9. Genesis 9:22-23** States, **"And ham, the father of Canaan, saw the nakedness of his father and told his two brothers outside. But Shem and Japheth took a garment, laid it on both their shoulder and went backwards and covered the nakedness of their father. Their faces were turned away, and they did not see their father's nakedness."**
Noah became drunk on wine and fell asleep naked in his tent, in full view of everyone. When Ham saw Noah in this state, instead of turning away or doing something to help his father, he went out and told his brothers about it. The way he told them about it was mocking and derisive and he showed no respect to his father whatsoever. Shem and Japheth on the other hand treated their father with decency and respect by covering him up so that no one else would see his shame. They knew that one of their responsibilities as sons is to respect their father. As a result of their actions they received blessings from Noah but Ham and his descendants were cursed.

The things that your servant of God is going through should not cause you to despise him. As Apostle Paul said in his letter to the church in Galatia in **Galatians 4:14 "And my trial which was in my flesh you did not despise or reject, but you received me as an**

angel of God, even as Christ Jesus." No matter what he is going through he was chosen by God and his anointing is still upon him. That should be your primary focus.

In **2 Kings 2**, Elisha's primary focus was on Elijah's anointing and not on anything that the prophet had done in the past that caused God to call him home. All the other sons of the prophet knew that Elijah's time was up and had probably speculated as to the reason why he was being taken home. We are told that as Elijah was embarking on his final journey, Elisha refused to leave him. In **2 Kings 2:1-12**, Elijah tried to get rid of Elisha three times but each time he refused to stay behind and insisted on accompanying the prophet. Elijah went from Gilgal to Bethel, from Bethel to Jericho and from Jericho of Jordan with Elisha following him all the way. In each of these locations, there were other sons of the prophet who world try to discourage Elisha. An example is in **2 Kings 2:5** which states, **"Now the sons of the prophets who were at Jericho came to Elisha and said to him, 'Do you know that the LORD will take away your master from over you today?' So he answered, 'Yes, I know keep silent'"** Elisha did not want the chartering of the sons of the prophet to distract him from his main goals. He was determined to accompany Elijah to the very end and to get the double portion of his anointing. You too must learn to be like Elisha and not let the chattering and murmuring of other people distract you from your main focus. In your walk with God, you will come across a lot of distracters, seeking to move you away from the presence of God. They are present everywhere in your office, your home and especially in the church. You must learn to tell them to mind their own business just like Elisha told the other sons of the prophet.

Regardless of how bad the church has become today, you still need it. **Romans 10:17** states that faith comes by hearing the word of God and it is in the church that you will hear the word. The bible says that we should not despise the gathering of the children of God and so you have to look beyond all the politics that is present in the church today and focus on the truth that is being preached there.

While the servant of God might be the first person that the enemy will use to try to remove you from God's presence, Satan will also use the behaviour of other people in the church to distract you. Sometimes people who are supposed to be leaders in the church like workers, deacons and assistant pastors act in a manner that is very discouraging to members of the congregation. They come late to church, they do not attend special services and they do not set a good example for the rest of the congregation. You should leave them to God because they too are only human and many of them are struggling with the responsibilities that they have been given. If however, they do not meet God's expectations for their lives, then he will reward them according to the works of their hands and not according to the work titles or the positions that they held. **Matthew 19:30** states, **"But many who are first will be last, and the last first."** If you find someone's attitude particularly districting or reprehensible, then you should take the person to God in prayer. Hand over the matter to him and let him deal with it in the way that he sees fit but do not let that person's actions remove you from the presence of God.

You have to be very careful who and what you listen to because Satan has many agents in the most unlikely places seeking to sow seeds of discord in the house of God. One of my spiritual son's and I had a falling out because he was not willing to listen to instructions and to hear the truth. When he decided to leave the church, he went about saying all sorts of things about me to the members of my congregation. This man was a minister and people knew that he was close to me, so when he started speaking negatively about me, some people listened and believed that there must be some element of truth in his accusations. When he came back to apologise to me sometime after, I brought him out in front of the entire congregation so that everyone would hear what he had to say. I did this so that the people he had spoken to could hear from the horse's mouth that there was no truth in what he had told them. If anyone allowed the lies this man told to take them away from the presence of God they only have themselves to blame.

Even servants of God have to make such that they look beyond the church. If you have a calling upon your life, do not look at the behaviour of other servants of God and allow them to prevent you from being who God created you to be. As I stated in a previous chapter, nowadays there are many Bishops, Pastors and Evangelists who are bringing reproach to the Lord. Some who have been called by God to serve him do not want to be associated with such people and so they refuse to heed the call. If this is your situation, you must not allow other people to render you useless to the lord. Do not allow the actions and attitudes of anyone else to affect our relationship with God.

Servants of God should also not allow the behaviour and attitudes of the members of their congregation to discourage them. Sometimes you may get frustrated when the word you are ministering is not getting through to people, when you see that despite all your effort their attitudes have not changed you may be tempted to throw in the towel and therefore fail in the task that the Lord has set you. There are times when I get so discouraged by people's behaviour that I want to just leave everything behind and stay on my own with my family. I have had to apologise to the Lord in the past for this kind of attitude. If a servant of God does not look beyond his congregation he too will miss it. Moses did not get to see the Promised Land because he allowed the attitude of the children of Israel to cause him to sin.

No matter what your position in the church is, therefore you must look beyond the church, look beyond the servant of God, the ministers and the members of the congregation. Place your focus on the word that is being spoken and on the truth in it. Do not allow yourself to be distracted or discouraged by what anyone else does rather concentrate on making heaven at all costs. The race for heaven is a personal one; it is not a congregational race, or is it a race that you run with anyone else. Your father and mother, your spouse or your children, none of them run the race with you. You cannot, therefore, allow any of them to prevent you from making heaven.

Chapter 7

DEAL WITH WORLDLINESS

This world we live in today is an evil system, controlled by the devil **(1 John 5:19)**. The bible states in **James 4:4** that **"friendship with the world is enmity with God."** It, therefore, follows that love of the world or worldliness is something that we must avoid if we want to make heaven.

1 John 2:15-16 states, **"Do not love the world or the things in the world. If any loves the world, the love of the father is not in him. For all that is in the world the lust of the flesh, the lust of the eyes, and the pride of life is not of the Father but is of the world."**

From this passage, we see that worldliness is internal and starts from the heart. **1 John 2:16** breaks down the things that worldliness consists of as the lust of the flesh, the lust of the eyes and the pride of life. The New International Version of the Bible translates this phrase as, **"The cravings of sinful man, the lust of his eyes and the boasting of what he has and does."**

The lust of the flesh describes the desire to satisfy our base appetites and passions at all costs. It is the lust for physical pleasure and the desire to indulge our sensual nature. The lust of the eyes refers to greed and desire for things that entice the eyes, such as luxurious or opulent items, while the pride of life is an assurance in one's resources and abilities. It can be found in someone who glories in himself or his possessions. If we are to make heaven, no trace of worldliness can be found in us, we must let go of the world. Our vanity must go and our reliance on our abilities and resources must be replaced by a total reliance on the Most High God.

The bible provides us with many examples of people who allowed worldliness to take them away from the presence of God. The very first illustration of the disastrous effects that worldliness can have on the life of man can be found in **Genesis 3**. It was Eve's worldliness, the lust of the eyes, which brought about man's original sin.

Genesis 3:6 states, "**So when the woman saw that the tree was good for food, that it was pleasant to the eyes, and a tree desirable to make one wise, she took of its fruit and ate. She also gave to her husband with her, and he ate.**"

The serpent used the lust of the eyes that he saw in Eve to entice her to eat the fruit of the tree of life. God had created Eve to be a helpmate to Adam but instead of fulfilling her role, she became the architect of his downfall. She broke the relationship that Adam had with God and took him out of God's perfect will because of her worldliness.

In **Genesis's 39:1-20**, we read the account of Joseph's experience as a slave in the house of Potiphar. Joseph had found grace and favour in Potiphar's eyes and had assumed a lot of the responsibilities of his household. The bible also tells us in **Genesis 39:5** that the Lord Blessed Potiphar's house because of Joseph. Potiphar's wife became overcome with desire for Joseph and wanted to sleep with him. When he refused, she manipulated her husband into putting Joseph into prison. It follows that when Joseph left Potiphar's household, the blessings of the Lord also departed with him. Potiphar's wife allowed her worldliness, the lust of the flesh, to make her husband lose his blessings.

Many women who are supposed to be agents of blessings to their husbands and whose primary role is to ensure that their husbands fulfil their divine purpose here on earth have like Eve and Potiphar's wife, allowed their worldliness, the lust of the eyes, the lust of the flesh and the pride of life to destroy their husbands. A woman's greatest accomplishment may be to help her husband

and children accomplish great things in life. It, therefore, follows that her greatest failure will be to prevent them from doing so.

Most women have a natural ability to manipulate; they have the ear of their husband and can often make him do what they want. A good woman will be a blessing to her husband and can help him become who the Lord created him to be. This is why **Proverbs, 18:22** says, **"he who finds a wife finds a good thing, and obtained favour from the LORD."** Many women, however, are using their gifts to bring about destruction to their husbands and their homes. They have allowed worldliness to consume them and rather than being a blessing they have like Eve, become the architects of their husband's downfall. Women need to examine themselves very carefully to determine the driving force in their lives. If they are motivated by the love of God then they and their household will prosper. If however they are ruled by a love of the things of this world, then they and their households will be destroyed.

Another illustration of how worldliness can destroy a life can be found in the life of king Asa. In **2 Chronicles 14,** we are introduced to King Asa who ascended to the throne after the death of his father King Abijah, **2 Chronicles 14:2-4** states, **"Asa did what was good and right in the eyes of the Lord his God for he removed the altars of the foreign gods and the high places, and broke down the sacred pillars and cut down the wooden images. He commanded Judah to seek the Lord God of their father, and to observe the law and the commandment."**

At the start of Asa's reign as king of Judah, he relied on God for everything. He did what was right in the eye of God by removing the altars where the people worshipped idols and commanded them to serve the Most High God faithfully. When Zerah the Ethiopian attacked Judah with an army that was more than twice the size of Judah's army, Asa called on the Lord for help **2, Chronicles 14:11** states, **"And Asa cried out to the LORD his God, and said, 'Lord it is nothing for you to help, whether with many or with those who have no power, help us, O LORD our God for we rest on you, and in your name, we go against this multitude. O LORD, you are our God; do not let man prevail against you!'"** Asa handed the battle over to the Lord and asked him to take control and the Lord answered his prayers and destroyed the Ethiopians.

After the Lord granted Judah victory over the Ethiopians, prophet Azariah brought king Asa a message from God. **2 Chronicles 15:2** states, **"And he went out to meet Asa, and said to him "Hear me Asa, and all Judah and Benjamin. The lord is with you while you are with him. If you seek him, he will be found by you but if you forsake him, he will forsake you."**

Azariah came to speak to king Asa out of the blue. Judah had just recorded a great victory against a mighty army, it had acquired a lot of material possessions to swell its coffers and there was peace in the land. Most importantly, King Asa had done a lot to make sure that the whole of Judah stopped worshipping idols and was faithful to the Lord, you could say that Azariah's warning was coming at a peculiar time because everything was going well in Judah. Sometimes when the servant of God comes to speak to you, even though nothing negative has happened in your life, be careful and take note of what he tells you. The Lord has seen ahead of you and knows what the enemy is planning against you.

Jesus saw ahead of time that Satan was going to tempt Peter and he warned him so that he would be on his guard. **Luke 22:31-34 "And the Lord said, "Simon, Simon! Indeed, Satan has asked for you, that he may sift you as wheat, "But I have prayed for you, that your faith should not fall; and when you have returned to Me, strengthen your brethren. "But he said to him, "Lord, I am ready to go with you, both to prison and to death." Then he said, "I tell you, Peter, the rooster shall not crow this day before you will deny three times that you know me."**

When Jesus warned Peter of the danger to come, Peter's response shows that he thought Jesus' warning was not required. He believed that given his relationship with Jesus nothing and no one could ever cause him to deny him. We should be careful when we dismiss the warning of the Lord as unnecessary and when we believe that we are stronger than we are. The bible says **1 Corinthians 10:12 "Therefore let him who thinks he stands take heed lest he fall."**

We are not told how seriously King Asa took Azariah's message not to forsake God, but he was certainly inspired to carry out even more reforms in the land of Judah. The things that he did pleased the Lord and as a result, Judah prospered and was at peace for many years. When people saw that Judah was prospering, they wanted to be a part of the property and many people from other tribes came to join Judah. When the Lord is prospering you, many people will flock around you. You must be very careful when this happens because the people who come around when you are doing well could eventually become the cause of your downfall. If people begin to tell you how wonderful you are, it could get to your head and most times will lead you to behave in a manner that is displeasing to the Lord. When this happens, then the lord will depart from your life and the people whose praising caused your downfall will also flee.

It seems that the year of peace and prosperity and the various alliances he made caused King Asa to forget who his real source was. In **2 Chronicles 16**, we read that King Baasha of Israel began to make moves to attack Judah. In the past, king Asa would have asked the lord for help but this time he did not. Instead, he turned to Ben-Hadad, King of Syria and allied with him so that the Syrian's could help Judah defeat Israel. To gain Syria's co-operation, king Asa gave Ben-Hadad silver and gold from the house of the Lord and the Syrian's fought Israel on Judah's behalf and defeated them.

What do we make of king Asa's failure to call on the Lord for help? Before God prospered king Asa, he had no resources and no one to call on for help whenever he was under attack. In those times, he placed his full trust in the Lord and the Lord defeated all his enemies. Once he gained material resources and connections, however, he ceased to put his trust in the Lord and began to rely on the things that he had acquired and the connections he had made. The pride of life, one of the symptoms of worldliness consumed him, and he forgot the warning that prophet Azariah gave him years earlier about not forsaking the Lord. When we rely on God in everything that we do, we give him honour and show just how much we love him. By placing our trust in other things or other people, we are showing disdain for the Lord and provoking his anger.

The Lord instructed Hanani the prophet to tell King Asa that he has failed him by relying on man and on his riches instead of turning to the Most High God. In **2 Chronicles 16:7-9,** Hanani reminded king Asa that it was the Lord who had defeated Judah's enemies in the past. He informed King Asa that because of his sins, peace would no longer reign in Judah. Instead of king Asa repenting and asking the Lord for forgiveness, he grew angry and threw the prophet in jail. In **2 Chronicles 16:12-14**, we read that the Lord afflicted king Asa with a severe sickness from which he eventually died. We are not told that king Asa ever repented of his sins and as a result, he will have ended up in hell. King Asa lost everything because he had been consumed by worldliness. His power and wealth blinded him to the truth of what he had become. At the end of the day, his good beginnings did not count for anything and hell became his eternal dwelling place.

Many of us commit the same sins as King Asa. Before the Lord blesses us, we have no one to turn to but him. We have time to pray and seek His face and pour all our troubles out to him. The moment he answers us, however, and begins to bless us, we forget where we came from and who was responsible for our prosperity. We begin to spend more time on the things of the world instead of the things of God and before we know it, we would have left the presence of God.

In **Matthew 19:16-30**, we read the story about the rich young man, who asked Jesus what he needed to do to make heaven. Jesus told him in **Matthew 19:21** that if he wanted to be perfect, he should sell everything that he had, give it to the poor and follow Him.

Matthew 19:22-24, states, **"Then Jesus said to his disciples, "Assuredly, I say to you that it is hard for a rich man to enter the kingdom of heaven. And again I say to you, it is easier for a camel to go through the eye of a needle than for a rich man to enter the kingdom of God".**

It is very difficult for a rich man to be saved because he has a lot to struggle with. Money comes into the life of a man like a serpent, it talks to him, makes him feel that he is important and worthy and deserving. It makes him think more of himself and his abilities than he ought to and eventually leads him to destruction.

Matthew 6:19-24, "Do not lay up for yourselves treasures on earth, where moth and rust destroy and where thieves break in and steal; but lay up for yourselves treasures in heaven, where neither moth nor rust destroys and where thieves do not break in and steal. "For where your treasure is, there your heart will be also. "The lamp of the body is the eye. If therefore your eye is good, your whole body will be full of light. "But if your eye is bad, your whole body will be full of darkness. If therefore the light that is in you is darkness, how great is that darkness! "No one can serve two masters; for either he will hate the one and love the other, or else he will be loyal to the one and despise the other. You cannot serve God and mammon."

We invest so much in acquiring material things in this world and ignore where we are supposed to spend eternity. At the end of the day, we cannot take anything with us when we go. Jesus said in **Luke 14:34** that whoever does not forsake everything that he has cannot be his disciple. If you say you are a Christian but you are not ready to give up all you have for the sake of your salvation, then you are not a Christian. When it comes to your Christianity, your money, wealth and power must be irrelevant. For as long as you allow the things that you possess to motivate you and influence the decisions that you make, you will not make heaven. This does not mean that you should not have money or position; rather it means that your money and position should have no part to play when it comes to obedience to the commandments of God. Until we get to this level, worldliness is still in us and if we are still worldly, then heaven is an impossibility.

Using the three keys of worldliness, Satan tempted Jesus, our ultimate role model. He tempted him the first time using the lust of the flesh in **Matthew 4:3** when he asked Jesus to use his power to turn a stone into a loaf of bread, Jesus was hungry and weak and after fasting for forty days, he chose not to use his divine power to satisfy his natural desire for food.

Satan tempted Jesus the second time with the pride of life in **Matthew 4:6**, telling Him that if He was indeed the son of God, He should jump down from the mountain. Jesus could have tried to prove that indeed he was the son of God, he had the power and therefore he would jump but he did not jump.

In **Matthew 4:9**, the final temptation using the lust of the eyes, he showed Jesus all the kingdoms of the world and their glory and told him that if He bowed down before him, he would give them all to Jesus. Again, Jesus refused to bow down to Satan's temptation. He was able to resist Satan's temptation because He knew the Word of God and He obeyed it.

Whenever you are being tempted remember that Jesus was also tempted yet he did not sin. Satan will try to use the things of this world to cause you to miss heaven but you can choose whether or not to fall. If you succumb to the lust of the eyes, the lust of the flesh and the pride of life then you will have written your ticket to hell.

We are all the architects of our destiny. What we do today will determine where we will end up tomorrow. Let us examine our lives very carefully. If we allow worldliness to rule our lives and take us to hell, then we only have ourselves to blame. However, if we let go of worldliness and begin to thirst after the things of God knowing full well that everything in this world is only temporary, then we will make it to heaven.

Chapter 8

CONCLUSION

Heaven should be the ultimate goal for every child of God. God has prepared it for us as a place of eternal rest and fellowship with him. In heaven, there is only peace and joy and we will encounter none of the sufferings that we do here on earth. Why then are children of God not focused on making heaven?

In the parable of the wedding banquet that we looked at in **Luke 14:16-24**, the guests gave various excuses for not being able to attend the banquet. In the same way, we give God excuses for focusing on the things of this world, instead of on him. In **Matthew 6:33**, God commands us to seek his kingdom and his righteousness before anything else and no excuse can even justify not doing so.

If we want to qualify to make heaven, we must be born again Christians in the sense of God's understanding of the term. This means that we must no longer conform to the ways of this world but become new beings with ideologies, beliefs and attitudes that are not of this world but of the kingdom of heaven. We must not blend in with the world rather we must stand out and let the light of our lives transform the darkness around us.

We must also recognize that the race for heaven is a personal one and we should not allow ourselves to be distracted or discouraged by the things or people that are around us. We must look beyond the politics and controversies that are present in our churches today and focus instead on the truth in the word of God that we are hearing.

The final thing that we must do if we want to make heaven, is to get rid of any trace of worldliness that is still in us. We must examine our lives very carefully to make sure that the lust of the flesh, the lust of the eyes and the pride of life are not controlling us. We must take our eyes off the things of this world and cease making the accumulation of wealth, position and power our primary focus.

As much as God wants us all to make heaven, he will not compromise His standards for us. Before we can qualify to inhabit the mansions He has prepared for us, we must do all that he asks, no matter how inconvenient it may be. At the end of the day, we must remember that life is a journey. Earth is only our temporary abode and we must not allow ourselves to be distracted, otherwise, we will not make heaven.

Pastor Seyi Ogunorunyinka, a minister of the Gospel, is anointed and gifted in healing and deliverance, spiritual warfare and in the power of the Holy Spirit. A prophet called by GOD and being used to release empowerment for abundance and victory in the lives of believers. Through his ministry, lives are being touched daily with the power of the Holy Spirit leading to peace and restoration to GOD's abundant life.

Pastor Seyi Ogunorunyinka is the Pastor of the Promised Land Restoration Ministries (PLRM) based in Lagos, Nigeria. PLRM is a ministry standing on the truth of GOD'S word and whose vision is propelled by the Holiness and Righteousness of GOD.

9 798417 653957